THE RESOURCE FOR
SMALL GROUP WORSHIP

THE RESOURCE FOR SMALL GROUP WORSHIP

VOLUME TWO

Devised by
Chris Bowater

Kevin Mayhew

First published in 2000 by
KEVIN MAYHEW LTD
Buxhall
Stowmarket
Suffolk IP14 3BW

ISBN 184003 511 0
ISMN M57004 668 3
Catalogue No. 1450171

Illustrations by E. Margaret Inkpen
Cover design by Jonathan Stroulger
Edited by Helen Elliot
Project Co-ordinator: Asher Gregory

Printed in Great Britain

Important Copyright Information Regarding the Songs in this Book

Creative Team

Devised by Chris Bowater

Editorial	E. Margaret Inkpen & Carol Woodcock
Writers	Jane Amey, E. Margaret Inkpen, Jo Pimlott, Pat Turner
Illustrations	E. Margaret Inkpen
Audio	Laurie Blackler & Daniel Bowater

Recorded at dB Studios, Lincoln

The Resource for Small Group Worship has been devised with convenience, variety and flexibility in mind. Taking into account also the breadth of worship experience and expression, this resource seeks to provide creative opportunities for 'all-age worship' without being either too condescending or too academic.

Contents

How to Use
The Resource for Small Group Worship

Convenience For the all-too-busy group leader, this resource provides a complete worship experience that includes:

- Worship songs: gently contemporary, easy to follow without being predictable.
- Meditation: wordless worship, a time to pause, reflect, consider and listen to God.
- Bible readings: arranged for corporate, responsive or personal reading.
- Prayers: written in non-religious language, for corporate or personal use.
- Discussion topics: touching issues of faith, essentials of life, challenges in society.
- Creative activities: always fun, never too exclusive, certain to build group relationships.

Each worship session comes in two parts:

1 The Notes for Leader preparation section, which comprises:
   - an introduction to the theme
   - a list of resources required
   - notes for leading the session, with extracts from
   - relevant books and materials for further activities.

2 Worship Session material. The following icons are used to identify each section of the worship material or format. *Only pages with a large underlying icon may be photocopied, or pages of artwork to be used by the group*:

(O) Opening words (including worship song)

(M) Meditation and listening to God

(R) Reading from the Bible

(P) Prayer and praise (including worship songs)

Further activities, discussion, study and creative ideas

 Closing words

A full programme would take about 1 hour to complete.

Variety In order to provide as wide a range of material as possible, each volume of *The Resource for Small Group Worship* contains:

- three sessions of general worship

- one session aimed at families and children

- one session which focuses on social awareness and specific issues.

Flexibility *The Resource for Small Group Worship* can be used more selectively by leaders looking for:

- song selection

- meditation ideas

- thematic material

- specialist topics – e.g. social awareness, church festivals, seasonal issues, special occasions

- group activities – drama, craft-work and suchlike

- written prayers.

Though much of the groundwork has been done here for the group leader, the role of that leader is still crucial. Enlist the help of the Holy Spirit at all times so that the worship is truly 'in Spirit and truth'. Lead the people into an experience that more than fills a programme but also affects their homes, marriages, relationships, attitudes, and jobs: their whole lives.

May this resource be a blessing to you, your groups and churches.

Chris Bowater

SESSION 6

Notes for Leader

Session 6: General Worship

THEME: JESUS CHRIST, SON OF GOD

Introduction to theme

There is so much to learn about Jesus that it is difficult to know what to choose for study, but in worship there is no problem. Jesus is naturally the focus for our worship and praise! The group may question the depressing nature of Psalm 22, but it is so important to see the fulfilment of prophecy. God knew what was going to happen, and through the Spirit, David could put it into words. The end of the Psalm is so positive!

Consider the different ways of using the discussion material and choose the activity or presentation appropriate for your group and meeting. Some groups may include sharing in communion (bread and wine) during the worship, others may not. You could use bread and wine or the picture of Leonardo da Vinci's 'Last Supper' as visual aids.

Resources required

You will need enough copies of the session for your group.

Worship songs:

These will be found on Album 2, tracks 1-4.

 As we are gathered by John Daniels

 Jesus is King by Wendy Churchill

 Jesus, what a beautiful name by Tanya Riches

 Meditation track – *Pacem*

Copies of the phrases on pages 18 and 19; and answers, if needed, on pages 20-21.

 Optional – a picture of Leonardo da Vinci's 'Last Supper'.

 Optional bread and wine.

 Extract from *Breaking the Rules* by Eddie Askew, published by The Leprosy Mission International, 80 Windmill Road, Brentford, TW8 OQH.

Preparation

 Meditation and listening to God

The reading, an extract from *Breaking the Rules* by Eddie Askew, is shared by the leader and a group member who has been approached before the meeting and given an opportunity to study the poem.

Leader Leonardo da Vinci's painting of 'The Last Supper' is well known. It is a mural painted directly onto a wall. The twelve disciples are all grouped around Jesus on the far side of the table, and at each end. The near side, nearest the spectator, is empty. Nothing is obscured. You can see the faces of everyone involved.

The viewer can take his or her place at the table as a participant at the meal. There's a place at the table for us.

'This is my body, broken for you,' said Jesus. The host at the table invites us to join him.

Group member Lord, I hardly dare accept
the invitation.
I want to sit with you
to hear your words

to share the meal.
To stretch across the table,
take the bread and wine
straight from your hands.

I want to join the others
grouped around you.

Offering your body.
Coarse ground
between the millstones of rejection.
Your blood, trod out,
beneath shod feet
which trample, unconcerned
on holiness.

I'd settle for much less, Lord
some slight acknowledgement
in passing,
that you care
but not the lengths to which you go
to show your love.

The leader can place a loaf of bread and a glass of wine on a central table as a visual reminder, or the group might wish to continue with sharing communion after a time of meditation.

Suggested time for meditation: 3-5 minutes.

To close

Leader For God so loved the world that he gave his one and only Son that whoever believes in him should not perish, but have eternal life.

Before moving on allow time for the group to share any thoughts arising from the time of meditation.

Prayer and Praise

The short prayers, provided for use by members of the group, could be cut into individual sections and placed centrally, where they are easily accessible, or given to individuals (see page 23).

 Further activities

Start the discussion by giving the numbered list of responses below to members of the group to read in turn, after the introduction. The order is not significant (see page 32).

Introduction: There is still a great deal of controversy about Jesus. Not necessarily what he did, or that he actually existed, because these are historical facts; but who he was. It is seen as extraordinary that a relatively young man, in a period of three years, could generate such contradictory and impassioned opinions from the general public with whom he came face to face. Let's read the list of reactions in turn.

The references on pages 18-19 look at the responses of people in various situations during Jesus' ministry and life. Encourage the group to focus on the events and the responses, how people were affected by what happened, and how this might give us insight into the reactions of people today. If we live as Jesus taught in the Gospels, we should expect the same reactions. Do we?

Optional activity

The following discussion/activity can be developed in a number of different ways:

a) The leader can use the references and material for a talk, with discussion or questions.

b) The group can divide into twos or threes with copies of the reference list provided, pages 18 and 19, using Bibles to find the answers.

c) The list of answers on pages 20 and 21 can be cut into sections, and small groups decide which are the appropriate answers to the questions without the use of Bibles. They will need glue, and copies of the reference list.

Reactions to Jesus

Look up each reference and write down the reaction, or response, given for each situation. If you have time you may want to continue looking up more situations and responses to add to the list.

	Situation	Reaction/Response
1	Example Matthew 17:5-6 The Transfiguration What was the reaction of Peter, James and John?	They were terrified.
2	Mark 10:21-22 What was the response of the rich young man?	
3	Luke 7:36-39 What was the response of Simon, the Pharisee?	
4	Luke 7:6-7 What was the centurion's statement to Jesus?	
5	Luke 23:47/ Mark 15:39 What was the response of the centurion at the cross?	
6	Luke 8:25 What was the disciples' response to Jesus' calming the storm?	
7	Matthew 13:54-58 What was the reaction of local people in Jesus' hometown?	

	Situation	Reaction/Response
8	John 11:17-22, 27, 32-37 What were the responses of Mary, Martha and the other people on the death of Lazarus?	
9	Luke 17:15-16 What was the response of the Samaritan leper?	
10	Luke 23:32-33, 39-42 What were the responses of the criminals crucified with Jesus?	
11	John 11:45-48 What was the response of the Chief Priests and Pharisees?	
12	Matthew 2:1-2, 11 What was the reaction of the wise men when they found Jesus with his parents?	
13	John 12:12-13 What was the reaction of the people to Jesus on his way to Jerusalem?	
14	John 13:5-6, 8-9 What were the two responses of Peter when Jesus washed his feet?	
15	Luke 7:37, 38 What did the woman do to show her love of Jesus?	

Reactions to Jesus - References and Answers

	Situation	Reaction/Response
1	**Example** Matthew 17:5-6 The Transfiguration What was the reaction of Peter, James and John?	They were terrified.
2	Mark 10:21-22 What was the response of the rich young man?	His face fell. He went away sad.
3	Luke 7:36-39 What was the response of Simon, the Pharisee?	If he were a prophet he would know who is touching him and what kind of woman she is.
4	Luke 7:6-7 What was the centurion's statement to Jesus?	I do not deserve to have you come under my roof. I did not consider myself worthy to come to you. Just say the word and my servant will be healed.
5	Luke 23:47/ Mark 15:39 What was the response of the centurion at the cross?	Surely this was the Son of God.
6	Luke 8:25 What was the disciples' response to Jesus' calming the storm?	In fear and amazement they asked one another, 'Who is this?'
7	Matthew 13:54-58 What was the reaction of local people in Jesus' hometown?	Where did he get this wisdom and these miraculous powers? They were amazed and offended.
8	John 11:17-22, 27, 32-37 What were the responses of Mary, Martha and the other people on the death of Lazarus?	If you had been here, our brother would not have died. I believe you are the Christ. Mary fell at Jesus' feet weeping. Could he not have kept this man from dying? See how he loved him.

	Situation	Reaction/Response
9	Luke 17:15-16 What was the response of the Samaritan leper?	He praised God with a loud voice. He threw himself at Jesus' feet and thanked him.
10	Luke 23:32-33, 39-42 What were the responses of the criminals crucified with Jesus?	Are you not the Christ? Save yourself and us. This man has done nothing wrong.
11	John 11:45-48 What was the response of the Chief Priests and Pharisees?	If we let him go on like this, everyone will believe in him and then the Romans will come and take away both our place (temple) and our nation.
12	Matthew 2:1-2, 11 What was the reaction of the wise men when they found Jesus with his parents?	They bowed down and worshipped him. Then they opened their treasures and presented him with gifts.
13	John 12:12-13 What was the reaction of the people to Jesus on his way to Jerusalem?	They waved palm branches and went to meet him, shouting 'Hosanna!'
14	John 13:5-6, 8-9 What were the two responses of Peter when Jesus washed his feet?	'No, Lord, you shall never wash my feet.' 'Then, Lord, not just my feet, but my hands and head as well.'
15	Luke 7:37, 38 What did the woman do to show her love of Jesus?	She stood behind him weeping, and wet his feet with her tears, she wiped them with her hair, kissed them and poured perfume on them.

Worship Session 6

THEME: JESUS CHRIST, SON OF GOD

Opening words

> **Leader** For God so loved the world that he gave his one and only Son that whoever believes in him shall not perish, but have everlasting life.
> (John 3:16)

> **Group** *His name is Immanuel, meaning 'God with us'.*
> *Amen. Come, Lord Jesus.*
> *(Matthew 1:23; Revelation 22:20)*

> **Leader** On the evening of that first day of the week, when the disciples were all together, Jesus came and stood among them, and said 'Peace be with you!'
> (John 20:19)

> **Group** *His name is Immanuel, meaning 'God with us'.*
> *Amen. Come, Lord Jesus.*

> **Leader** Jesus said, 'Where two or three come together in my name, there am I with them.'
> (Matthew 18:20)

Worship song

As we are gathered
John Daniels

As we are gathered, Jesus is here;
one with each other, Jesus is here;
joined by the Spirit, washed in the blood,
part of the body, the Church of God.
As we are gathered, Jesus is here;
one with each other, Jesus is here.

Reading from the Psalms

Leader My God, my God, why have you forsaken me?
        Why are you so far from saving me,
        so far from my words of groaning?
        O my God, I cry out by day but you do not answer;
        by night, and am never silent.

Group *Yet you are enthroned as the Holy One;*
       You are the praise of Israel.
       In you our fathers put their trust;
       they trusted and you delivered them.
       They cried to you and were saved;
       in you they trusted and were not disappointed.

Leader But I am less than a man,
        scorned by men and despised by the people.
        All who see me mock me;
        they hurl insults, shaking their heads, saying:
        'He trusts in the Lord; let the Lord rescue him.
        Let him deliver him, since he delights in him.'

Group *Yet you brought me out of the womb;*
       you made me trust you even at my mother's breast.
       From birth I was cast upon you,
       from my mother's womb you have been my God.
       Do not be far from me, for trouble is near
       and there is no one to help.

Leader I am poured out like water,
        all my bones are out of joint.
        My heart has turned to wax;
        it has melted away within me.
        Evil men have encircled me;
        they have pierced my hands and my feet.
        I count all my bones; people stare and gloat over me.

They divide my garments among them
and cast lots for my clothing.

Group *But you, O Lord, be not far off;*
O my Strength, come quickly to help me.
He has not despised or disdained the suffering of the
afflicted one;
He has not hidden his face from him,
but has listened to his cry for help.

Leader All the ends of the earth
will remember and turn to the Lord,
and all the families of the nations
will bow down before him.

Group *Future generations will be told about the Lord;*
they will proclaim his righteousness to a people yet
unborn – for he has done it! Amen.
(From Psalm 22)

Leader A psalm written many years before Jesus died on the
cross, by someone who had no idea what would happen – amazing prophetic words.

'All the ends of the earth will remember and turn to the
Lord . . . He has done it.'

Group *His name is Immanuel, God with us.*
Amen. Come, Lord Jesus.

Meditation and listening to God

The meditation is based on an extract from *Breaking the Rules* by Eddie Askew.

To close

Leader For God so loved the world that he gave his one and only Son that whoever believes in him should not perish, but have eternal life.

Prayer and praise

Members of the group can use the following prayers, or pray spontaneously, the focus of this time being on Jesus.

You came to earth as a baby, Lord Jesus,
and the name you were given by your Father meant
'One who saves his people from their sins'.
Thank you, Jesus, for being our Lord and Saviour.

Amen.

As a child, you spoke about your Father, Jesus.
Your teaching reveals the Father to us.
Thank you for showing us
that we can call him Father too.

Amen.

As a man,
you ate and walked and slept with your friends.
You laughed and talked and wept.
You were like one of us.
Thank you for sharing in our humanness,
and understanding people like me.

Amen.

Jesus, you cared for individuals,
yet you gave your life for the whole world.
You loved a rich young man, a tax collector,
a Roman centurion, a beggar, a leper,
the children and women like Mary and Martha.
You understood Peter and John.
They were your friends.
Thank you that each one of us can be special to you.

Amen.

Thank you, Lord Jesus,
for your miracles and healing power.
By your Holy Spirit, continue your work in us.

Amen.

Thank you for your words,
your teaching, and your stories, Jesus.
Without the Bible, we would be poor indeed.
Help us to share our knowledge about you with others.

Amen.

You died on the cross for our sake, Jesus.
You had the victory over death and rose again.
Help us to understand the meaning
of your death and resurrection.
Thank you for the new life we can have in you.

Amen.

Lord Jesus,
you are King of Glory, Prince of Peace!
We want to praise you
like the people who shouted 'Hosanna'
and waved palm branches in Jerusalem.
We worship you, Son of God, Lord and Saviour,
Redeemer and friend.

Amen.

Worship songs

Jesus is King
Wendy Churchill

Jesus is King and I will extol him,
give him the glory and honour his name.
He reigns on high, enthroned in the heavens,
Word of the Father, exalted for us.

We have a hope that is steadfast and certain,
gone through the curtain and touching the throne.
We have a Priest who is there interceding,
pouring his grace on our lives day by day.

We come to him, our Priest and Apostle,
clothed in his glory and bearing his name,
laying our lives with gladness before him;
filled with his Spirit we worship the King.

O holy One, our hearts do adore you,
thrilled with your goodness we give you our praise.
Angels in light with worship surround him,
Jesus, our Saviour, for ever the same.

Jesus, what a beautiful name
Tanya Riches

Jesus, what a beautiful name.

Son of God, Son of Man,

Lamb that was slain.

Joy and peace, strength and hope,

grace that blows all fear away.

Jesus, what a beautiful name.

Jesus, what a beautiful name.

Truth revealed, my future sealed,

healed my pain.

Love and freedom, life and warmth,

grace that blows all fear away.

Jesus, what a beautiful name.

Jesus, what a beautiful name.

Rescued my soul, my stronghold,

lifts me from shame.

Forgiveness, security, power and love,

grace that blows all fear away.

Jesus, what a beautiful name.

Further activity

Leader There is still a great deal of controversy about Jesus. Not necessarily what he did, or that he actually existed, because these are historical facts; but who he was. It is seen as extraordinary that a relatively young man, in a period of three years, could generate such contradictory and impassioned opinions from the general public with whom he came face to face. These are some of the reactions:

1 He speaks with authority, not like our religious leaders!
2 He's mad. Put him away.
3 We never saw anything like this.
4 He's nothing but a peasant carpenter from Nazareth.
5 All spoke well of him and wondered at his gracious words.
6 He's demon-possessed. Silence him!
7 Can this be the Messiah?
8 A great prophet has risen among us. God has visited his people.
9 He's a blasphemer. Destroy him!
10 We can't arrest Him. No one ever spoke like this man.
11 He's a political traitor. Kill him!
12 I can find no fault in this man.
13 Truly, this was the Son of God.

Closing words

Leader Lord, may the way we live our lives affect those around us, so that their response is to turn to you and declare, you are the Son of God.

All Jesus, we declare today, that you are the Son of God. Amen.

As we are gathered

Words and Music: John Daniels

Jesus is King

Words and Music: Wendy Churchill

2. We have a hope that is steadfast and certain,
   gone through the curtain and touching the throne.
   We have a Priest who is there interceding,
   pouring his grace on our lives day by day.

3. We come to him, our Priest and Apostle,
   clothed in his glory and bearing his name,
   laying our lives with gladness before him;
   filled with his Spirit we worship the King.

4. O holy One, our hearts do adore you;
   thrilled with your goodness we give you our praise.
   Angels in light with worship surround him,
   Jesus, our Saviour, for ever the same.

Jesus, what a beautiful name

Words and Music: Tanya Riches

SESSION 7

Notes for Leader

Session 7: General Worship

THEME: PEACE

Introduction to theme

The focus on this session is the Hebrew word for peace, SHALOM, and its definition. It is important to understand that peace will never happen 'out there', between nations and races, in cities and communities, families and churches, unless we are committed to it in our own lives and relationships. We need to know God's meaning of peace.

Relationships are a big issue and it is suggested that the prayer time follows the discussion, to give time to bring these before God.

Resources required

You will need enough copies of the session for your group.

Worship songs:

These will be found on Album 2, tracks 5-8.

 *Our confidence is in the Lord* by Noel and Tricia Richards

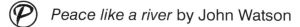 *Peace like a river* by John Watson

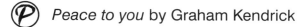 *Peace to you* by Graham Kendrick

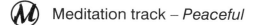 Meditation track – *Peaceful*

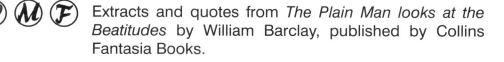 Extracts and quotes from *The Plain Man looks at the Beatitudes* by William Barclay, published by Collins Fantasia Books.

For optional activity (1)

- copies of the 'SHALOM' illustration
- felt pens, pencil crayons
- scissors and glue
- travel brochures, magazines to cut up.

 For activity (2)

- copies of Psalm 46, see page 47
- pens and pencils.

 For activity (3)

- copies of banner design, see page 48
- pens and pencils
- quote from *God is for Real, Man* by Carl Burke.

Preparation

 Opening words:

Introduce the session by reading this extract from *The Plain Man looks at the Beatitudes* by William Barclay:

For us peace can be largely a negative word; it tends to describe the absence or cessation of war or trouble. But for the Jew, peace had a far wider meaning. The Hebrew word is shalom. Shalom has two meanings. It can describe perfect welfare, serenity, prosperity and happiness – a condition of perfect and complete well being.

Secondly, it can describe right personal relationships; shalom means intimacy, fellowship, and uninterrupted goodwill between man and man . . . perfection of human relationships. Paul begins every letter with the prayer that grace and peace may be on the people to whom he writes.

Meditation and listening to God

Introduce the thought for meditation by reading this passage from William Barclay's *The Plain Man looks at the Beatitudes*:

Everyone knows that each person is a mixture, capable of good and evil . . . there is continual tension, continual inner debate. A man is a 'walking civil war'; never knowing which side within him will win the victory. Everyone longs for peace in the inner warfare of his own personality and his soul, and Jesus Christ is the only one who can make that peace. Something from outside oneself has to come in and take control.

Paul says, 'I no longer live, but Christ lives in me.'
(Galatians 2:20)

Psalm 37 says, 'The meek will . . . enjoy great peace'. The meek – those totally committed to God, under his control so they are at peace within themselves, at peace with other people, at peace with God. Those are the ones who enjoy great peace. The Prince of Peace lives in them.

Let's take a few moments to rest in the 'peace of God, which passes all understanding'.

Suggested time for meditation: 3-5 minutes.

To close

Leader The Lord bless you and keep you.
The Lord make his face shine upon you
and be gracious to you.
The Lord turn his face towards you and give you peace.

(Numbers 6:24-26)

Before moving on, allow time for the group to share any thoughts arising from the time of meditation.

Further activity

The following material (see pages 57-58) is based on William Barclay's *The Plain Man looks at the Beatitudes*, chapter 9, some of which has already been used in the worship period. A prayer time should follow the discussion, which looks at relationships. This seems appropriate as individuals may need time to think and pray about the areas of personal relationship which will be studied. *It is suggested that any activity be included before the discussion period* (see creative alternatives below).

After the introduction, read the following:

Barclay comments that,

We must mark one all-important fact in this Beatitude – the people to whom the blessing is promised. The people who are blessed are not 'peace lovers' but 'peacemakers' – those who break down barriers, not the ones who take the easy way out of trouble, or do nothing at all just to 'keep the peace'. Those who are blessed are prepared to face difficulty, unpopularity and trouble, to bring about peace. It is not by evading an issue but facing it, 'Shalom people' are involved in actively increasing the wellbeing and welfare of the world. They serve God by serving others. But this can only be done within a 'Shalom relationship'.

Similarly, between b) and c), quote from Barclay:

Herein is the task of the Christian . . . to labour to produce right relationships between man and man. In any society, in the private society of a home and in the public society of an institution or church, there are those who are disruptive influences and those who are reconciling influences, those who sow strife and those who sow peace.

and for c) read this passage:

Blessed indeed is the man who breaks down the barriers

between nation and nation, between man and man, and between man and God. Happy is the man whose life-work is the production of right relationships in every sphere of life. Such relationships can only enrich life when a man's own relationship with Jesus Christ is right.

 Optional creative activities

Your group may enjoy being creative while drinking coffee and sharing in fellowship. Activities 1 and 2 can be done in small informal groups, or individually with lots of discussion! Activity 3 is more serious.

Activity 1

Distribute copies of the 'SHALOM' illustration to those interested, with a selection of coloured felt pens or pencil crayons, and glue.

Encourage them to share a picture or place which comes to mind when they think of 'peace', for example, a lake, a sunset, a garden, a holiday location, a painting, a certain colour or music.

Provide travel brochures or magazines, and scissors. Pictures from these can be used to decorate the 'SHALOM' poster. A favourite verse about peace can be written in the space provided.

Activity 2

Distribute copies of the banner design, page 48, to small groups (twos or threes), with pens or pencils. On the back of the page, encourage people to write down the colours they would use, materials, decoration and additional wording.

(The group might even decide to make 'peace' banners for home, or the church meeting location!)

Activity 3

This will require more time and thought. Divide the group into twos, giving each pair a copy of Psalm 46. Ask them to rewrite the psalm in the language of today, referring to recent events, or in a more personal way.

This is an example of rewriting the psalm, from *God is for real, man* by Carl Burke:

God is a good hide-out; He is stronger than the weight lifter at the Y; . . . so what have you got to worry about, even if there's a flood, or the streets cave in and bridges get washed out?

Psalm 46

God is our refuge and strength,
an ever-present help in trouble.

Therefore we will not fear though the earth give way
and the mountains fall into the heart of the sea,
though its waters roar and foam
and the mountains quake with their surging.

There is a river whose streams make glad the city of God,
the holy place where the Most High dwells.

Nations are in uproar, kingdoms fall;
God lifts his voice, the earth melts.
The Lord Almighty is with us;
the God of Jacob is our fortress.

Come and see the works of the Lord.
He makes wars cease to the ends of the earth,
he breaks the bow and shatters the spear,
he burns the shields with fire.

Be still and know that I am God;
I will be exalted among the nations,
I will be exalted in all the earth.
The Lord Almighty is with us;
the God of Jacob is our fortress.

This is a design for a banner:

Banner Design

1 Choose your colours for:

a) background material

    _____

b) letters

    _____

c) other colours to be included

    _____

2 What else would you include in the design?

    _____

    _____

    _____

    _____

3 What other words might you add?

    _____

    _____

    _____

    _____

4 What materials would you use?

    _____

    _____

    _____

    _____

Worship Session 7

THEME: PEACE

Opening words

Leader God is our refuge and strength,
an ever-present help in trouble.
Be still and know that I am God.

The leader reads a passage from William Barclay's *The Plain Man looks at the Beatitudes*.

Leader Let's start our time together with a greeting of 'Shalom' – positive well being in the presence of God and perfect relationships with each other. 'Grace and peace to you from God our Father and the Lord Jesus Christ.'

Group *Shalom. God is our peace.*

The group can spend a few minutes sharing together with a handshake or hug, sharing a greeting of 'Shalom' – 'peace be with you'.

Worship song

Our confidence is in the Lord
Noel and Tricia Richards

Our confidence is in the Lord,
the source of our salvation.
Rest is found in him alone,
the Author of creation.
We will not fear the evil day,
because we have a refuge;
in every circumstance we say,
our hope is built on Jesus.

He is our fortress,
we will never be shaken.
He is our fortress,
we will never be shaken. (repeat)
We will put our trust in God.
We will put our trust in God.

Reading from the Psalms and the Book of Job

Leader　God is our refuge and strength,
　　　　　an ever-present help in trouble.

Group　*Therefore we will not fear*
　　　　　though the earth give way
　　　　　and the mountains fall into the heart of the sea,
　　　　　though its waters roar and foam
　　　　　and the mountains quake with their surging.

Leader　There is a river whose streams
　　　　　make glad the city of God,
　　　　　the holy place where the Most High dwells.

Group　*Nations are in uproar, kingdoms fall;*
　　　　　God lifts his voice, the earth melts.
　　　　　The Lord Almighty is with us;
　　　　　the God of Jacob is our fortress.

Leader　Come and see the works of the Lord.
　　　　　He makes wars cease to the ends of the earth,
　　　　　he breaks the bow and shatters the spear,
　　　　　he burns the shields with fire.

Group　*Be still and know that I am God;*
　　　　　I will be exalted among the nations,
　　　　　I will be exalted in all the earth.

Leader　The Lord Almighty is with us;
　　　　　the God of Jacob is our fortress.

　　　　　(From Psalm 46)

Group　*Shalom. God is our peace.*

Leader Submit to God and be at peace with him;
in this way prosperity will come to you.
Accept instruction from his mouth,
and lay up his words in your heart.

Group *If you return to the Almighty, you will be restored.*
Surely you will find delight in the Almighty
and will lift up your face to God.

Leader You will pray to him and he will hear you
and you will fulfil your vows.

Group *What you decide on will be done*
and light will shine on your ways.
(From Job 22)

Leader Submit to God, and be at peace with him.

Group *Shalom. God is our peace.*

Meditation and listening to God

The leader reads a passage from William Barclay's *The Plain Man looks at the Beatitudes*.

Paul says, 'I no longer live, but Christ lives in me.' (Galatians 2:20)

Psalm 37 says, 'The meek will . . . enjoy great peace.' The meek – those totally committed to God, under his control so they are at peace within themselves, at peace with other people, at peace with God. Those are the ones who enjoy great peace. The Prince of Peace lives in them.

Let's take a few moments to rest in the 'peace of God, which passes all understanding'.

To close

Leader The Lord bless you and keep you.
The Lord make his face shine upon you
and be gracious to you.
The Lord turn his face towards you and give you peace.
(Numbers 6:24-26)

Prayer and praise

Worship songs

Peace like a river
John Watson

Peace like a river,

love like a mountain,

the wind of your Spirit

is blowing everywhere.

Joy like a fountain,

healing spring of life;

come, Holy Spirit,

let your fire fall.

Peace to you
Graham Kendrick

Peace to you.

We bless you now

in the name of the Lord.

Peace to you.

We bless you now

in the name of the Prince of Peace.

Peace to you.

Peace to you.

Peace to you.

Peace to you.

Further activity

Introduction

Leader At the beginning of our worship we looked at the two meanings of the Jewish (Hebrew) word for peace, shalom - a sense of positive well being, and living in right relationships with each other. Using three headings, we will be discussing peace that comes from our relationship with ourselves, with one another and with God. To be 'at peace' is not a passive state, but one of activity. We have to work at making peace.

Matthew 5:9 says, 'Blessed are the peacemakers for they shall be called the children of God.'

a) Right relationship with oneself. Review the meditation passage.

References		
Galatians 2:20		Isaiah 32:17-18
Psalm 37:11		Isaiah 48:22
Proverbs 14:30		Micah 5:5
John 14:27		Galatians 5:22
John 16:33		Ephesians 2:13-18, 22

b) Right relationship with others. Look up the following references and discuss the suggested thoughts:

Genesis 11:1-9: Discuss the issues which divide nations and neighbours. Why did it happen?

Hebrews 12:4; 1 Thessalonians 5:13: Discuss the problems of 'living at peace with all people' in your own experience.

2 Corinthians 13:11: Discuss 'aiming for perfection, being of one mind' within the Church.

Mark 9:50: How can we work to bring 'peace' to situations in families, communities, etc?

Ephesians 2:14: Jesus is our peace. He has broken down barriers and hostility. He has made us 'one', where God lives by his Spirit. Do we see this working out in Christian relationships?

c) Right relationship with God.

Read and discuss:

Romans 5:1	2 Chronicles 14:1-2
2 Peter 3:14	Job 22:21
Isaiah 54:10	Leviticus 26:6
Judges 3:1, 3:30, 5:31, 8:28.	

- What are the conditions of peace?
- What must happen before peace is experienced?

Closing words

Leader To achieve peace there is work to be done, internally, within ourselves, and externally too – learning obedience to God's law and taking hold of the covenant; fighting against evil and corruption; praying earnestly; bringing peace into divided relationships . . . and the reward is 'to be called the children of God . . . those who are close to God's own heart'.

A time of prayer follows.

Our confidence is in the Lord

Words and Music: Noel and Tricia Richards

Peace like a river

Words and Music: John Watson

Peace to you

Words and Music: Graham Kendrick

SESSION 8

Notes for Leader

Session 8: General Worship

THEME: HOPE

Introduction to theme

Before the meeting starts, you may want to ask a few people to say what they 'hope for' during the coming months or year. Write down these 'hopes' and check them with the definition (page 85) at the beginning of your discussion. By the end of this session, it is *hoped* that people will have a clearer understanding of the response, 'My hope is in the Lord'. It is aimed at providing a firm foundation to Christian faith, the solid rock that gives strength and purpose to our lives.

I feel I have grown a couple of inches in height during the preparation of this worship session – I am standing on the Rock! I wonder if your group will feel the same?

Resources required

You will need enough copies of the session for your group.

Worship songs:

These will be found on Album 2, tracks 9-12.

 Salvation belongs to our God by Adrian Howard and Pat Turner

 Faithful One by Brian Doerksen

 The Lord's my shepherd from The Scottish Psalter

 Meditation track – *Hope*

Copies of the Bible verses for study and discussion (see pages 69-73 for this material).

 Large sheet of paper or acetate.

Preparation

 Meditation and listening to God

Read this poem from *No Strange Land* by Eddie Askew, published by The Leprosy Mission International, 80 Windmill Road, Brentford, TW8 0QH.

Lord, I live in hope.
A lovely word.
Not the cheap cliché that shrugs its shoulders,
smiles, and says, 'it'll be alright on the night'.
But a deep root that holds me firm
in the bedrock of your love
whatever comes.

I hope for hope, Lord.
The seeds of light
sown in darkness round your cross,
germinate and flower and fruit
in the fallow fields of my small life.
My hope starts in your death and resurrection.
Continues in the certainty of your presence.
Fulfils itself in the clear calm confidence
of final victory.

For now, I cling to hope's small seedling.
Vulnerable. Not yet full-grown.
Measuring each day
in the new leaves of little victories
and help me, Lord, often in small defeats.
But still I cling to hope
and know you walk with me.
Thank you, Lord.

Suggested time for meditation: 3-5 minutes.

Before moving on, allow time for the group to share any thoughts arising from the time of meditation concerning 'hope', for themselves or in their relationship with God.

To close

Leader We have this hope as an anchor for the soul, firm and secure. It enters the inner sanctuary behind the curtain, where Jesus, who went before us, has entered on our behalf.
(Hebrews 6:19-20)

 Prayer and praise

Prayers arising from the period of meditation can be offered spontaneously. Some members of the group may prefer to use the short prayers on pages 81-82, which can be copied, cut into individual sections and placed centrally where they are easily accessible.

 Further activity

Encourage the group to give their definitions of the word 'HOPE'.

• Ask for the opposite word to 'HOPE'.

• What would be a good definition of the word 'DESPAIR'?

• What is the difference between HOPE and FAITH?

With the above definition in mind, continue with the activity described below.

The New Testament references (pages 71-73) can be copied and distributed to small groups, each having a copy of the Old Testament headings (pages 69-70).

The small groups read the verses and decide under which Old Testament reference they should be included.

This exercise can be followed by discussion as each group shares their answers, based on the theme.

Alternatively, each New Testament verse can be given to one member of the group. The leader reads the headings (Old Testament verses) using overheads, or a large sheet of paper, asking people to read out verses for each heading, giving reasons for including them.

A checklist is provided for the leader, but this is not a competitive exercise; there are no right and wrong answers. Rather, this is a chance to share ideas and talk about 'hope' in a biblical context.

Old Testament References – Headings

1 Deuteronomy 1:21

See, the Lord your God has given you the land. Go up and take possession of it as the Lord, the God of your fathers, told you. Do not be afraid; do not be discouraged.

a)

b)

2 Deuteronomy 31:8

The Lord himself goes before you and will be with you; he will never leave you nor forsake you. Do not be afraid, do not be discouraged.

a)

b)

c)

3 Joshua 8:1

The Lord said to Joshua, 'Do not be afraid; do not be discouraged. Take the whole army with you, and go up and attack Ai. For I have delivered into your hands the king of Ai, his people, his city and his land.'

a)

b)

c)

4 1 Chronicles 22:11, 13

David speaking to Solomon, his son: 'Now, my son, the Lord be with you and may you have success and build the house of the Lord your God, as he said you would. You will have success if you are careful to observe the decrees and laws that the Lord gave Moses. Be strong and courageous.' (i.e. Do not be afraid or discouraged.)

a)

b)

c)

5 1 Chronicles 28:20

David to Solomon: 'Be strong and courageous, and do the work. Do not be afraid or discouraged, for the Lord God is with you. He will not fail you or forsake you until all the work for the service of the temple of the Lord is finished.'

a)

b)

6 Isaiah 33:2, 6

O Lord . . . be our strength every morning, our salvation in time of distress. (Do not be afraid or discouraged!) He will be the sure foundation for your times, a rich store of salvation and wisdom and knowledge. The fear of the Lord is the key to this treasure.

a)

7 Isaiah 52:8b, 9b, 10b

When the Lord returns to Zion, they will see it with their own eyes. The Lord has comforted his people, he has redeemed Jerusalem. All the ends of the earth will see the salvation of our God.

a)

b)

New Testament References

Philippians 1:6

Being confident of this, that he who began a good work in you will carry it on to completion until the day of Christ Jesus.

Matthew 7:24-25

Everyone who hears these words of mine and puts them into practice is like a wise man, who built his house on the rock. The rain came down, the streams rose, and the winds blew and beat against that house; yet it did not fall because it had its foundations on the rock.

1 John 5:19

We know that we are the children of God, and that the whole world is under the control of the evil one.

James 2:5

Has not God chosen those who are poor in the eyes of the world to be rich in faith and to inherit the kingdom he promised to those who love him?

John 14:16

I will ask the Father and he will give you another Coun-sellor to be with you for ever, the Spirit of Truth.

Acts 1:11b

This same Jesus, who has been taken into heaven, will come back.

Colossians 1:5

. . . faith and love spring from the hope that is stored up for you in heaven and that you have already heard about in the word of truth, the gospel.

1 Corinthians 3:16

Don't you know that you yourselves are God's temple and that God's Spirit lives in you?

Matthew 6:33

Seek first his kingdom and his righteousness, and all these things will be given to you as well.

1 Corinthians 3:11, 12, 14

No one can lay any foundation other than the one already laid, which is Jesus Christ. If any one builds on this foundation . . . his work will be shown for what it is . . . If what he has built survives, he will receive his reward.

John 16:33b

In this world you will have trouble. But take heart! I have overcome the world.

Titus 2:13

We wait for the blessed hope – the glorious appearing of our great God and Saviour, Jesus Christ, who gave himself to redeem us.

John 14:26

The Counsellor, the Holy Spirit . . . will remind you of everything I have said to you. Peace I leave with you; my peace I give you . . . do not be troubled and do not be afraid.

1 John 5:4-5

Everyone born of God overcomes the world. This is the victory that has overcome the world, even our faith. Who is it that overcomes the world? Only he who believes that Jesus is the Son of God.

Matthew 28:20b

Surely I am with you always to the very end of the age.

Old Testament References with New Testament References

Leader's checklist

1 Deuteronomy 1:21

See, the Lord your God has given you the land. Go in and take possession of it as the Lord, the God of your fathers, told you. Do not be afraid; do not be discouraged.

a) James 2:5

b) Matthew 6:33

2 Deuteronomy 31:8

The Lord himself goes before you and will be with you. He will never leave you or forsake you. Do not be afraid; do not be discouraged.

a) John 14:16

b) John 14:26

c) Matthew 28:20b

3 Joshua 8:1

The Lord said to Joshua, 'Do not be afraid; do not be discouraged. Take the whole army with you and go up and attack Ai. For I have delivered into your hands the king of Ai, his people, his city and his land.'

a) 1 John 5:19

b) 1 John 5:4-5

c) John 16:33b

4 1 Chronicles 22:11, 13

David speaking to Solomon, his son: 'Now, my son, the Lord be with you and may you have success and build the house of the Lord your God as he said you would. You will have success if you are careful to observe the decrees and the laws that the Lord gave Moses. Be strong and courageous.' (i.e. Do not be afraid or discouraged.)

a) Matthew 7:24-25

b) 1 Corinthians 3:11, 12, 14

5 1 Chronicles 28:20

David to Solomon: 'Be strong and courageous and do the work. Do not be afraid or discouraged, for the Lord your God is with you. He will not fail you or forsake you until all the work for the service of the temple of the Lord is finished.'

a) Philippians 1:6

b) 1 Corinthians 3:16

6 Isaiah 33:2, 6

'O Lord . . . be our strength every morning, our salvation in time of distress. (Do not be afraid or discouraged!) He will be the sure foundation for your times, a rich store of salvation and wisdom and knowledge. The fear of the Lord is the key to this treasure.'

a) Colossians 1:5

7 Isaiah 52:8, 9b, 10b

When the Lord returns to Zion, they will see it with their own eyes. The Lord has comforted his people, he has redeemed Jerusalem. All the ends of the earth will see the salvation of our God.

a) Acts 1:11b

b) Titus 2:13

Worship Session 8

THEME: HOPE

Opening words

Leader Hope that is seen is no hope at all.
Who hopes for what he already has?
But if we hope for what we do not yet have,
we wait for it patiently.
(Romans 8:24-25)

Group *My hope is in you, O Lord.*

Leader Praise be to the God and Father of our Lord Jesus Christ!
In his great mercy he has given us new birth
into a living hope,
through the resurrection of Jesus Christ from the dead
and into an inheritance that can never perish,
spoil or fade, kept in heaven for you.
(1 Peter 1:3-4)

Group *My hope is in you, O Lord.*

Leader As for me, I shall always have hope.
I will praise you more and more.
My mouth will tell of your righteousness,
of your salvation all day long,
though I know not its measure.
(Psalm 71:14-15)

Group *My hope is in you, O Lord.*
I will tell of your righteousness and of your salvation,
though I know not its measure.

Worship song

Salvation belongs to our God
Adrian Howard and Pat Turner

Salvation belongs to our God,
who sits on the throne,
and to the Lamb.
Praise and glory, wisdom and thanks,
honour and power and strength.

Be to our God for ever and ever,
be to our God for ever and ever,
be to our God for ever and ever.
Amen.

And we, the redeemed, shall be strong
in purpose and unity,
declaring aloud,
praise and glory, wisdom and thanks,
honour and power and strength.

Reading from the Psalms

Leader To you, O Lord, I lift up my soul;
in you I trust, O my God.
Do not let me be put to shame
nor let my enemies triumph over me.

Group *No one whose help is in you*
will ever be put to shame,
but they will be put to shame
who are treacherous without excuse.

Leader Show me your ways, O Lord,
teach me your paths.

Group *Guide me in your truth and teach me,*
for you are God my Saviour
and my hope is in you all day long.

Leader Remember, O Lord, your great mercy and love
for they are from old.

Group *Remember not the sins of my youth*
and my rebellious ways;
according to your love remember me,
for you are good, O Lord.

Leader Good and upright is the Lord;
therefore he instructs sinners in his ways.
He guides the humble in what is right
and teaches them his ways.

Group *All the ways of the Lord are loving and faithful*
for those who keep the demands of his covenant.

Leader The Lord confides in those who stand in awe of him.
He makes his covenant known to them.

Group *My eyes are ever on the Lord,*
for only he will release my feet from the snare.

Leader Guard my life and rescue me;
let me not be put to shame, for I take refuge in you.

Group *May integrity and uprightness protect me,*
because my hope is in you.

(From Psalm 25)

Leader The eyes of the Lord are on those who fear him;
on those whose hope is in his unfailing love.

Group *We wait in hope for the Lord;*
he is our help and our shield.
In him our hearts rejoice,
for we trust in his holy name.

Leader May your unfailing love rest upon us, O Lord,
even as we put our hope in you.

(From Psalm 33)

Meditation and listening to God

Reading from *No Strange Land* by Eddie Askew.

To close

Leader We have this hope as an anchor for the soul, firm and secure. It enters the inner sanctuary behind the curtain, where Jesus, who went before us, has entered on our behalf.

(Hebrews 6:19-20)

Prayer and praise

Prayers or thoughts arising from the period of meditation or readings can be offered spontaneously. Some members of the group may prefer to use the short prayers provided:

Lord, God, in you I put my hope.
I have confidence in your word.
I believe in Jesus – the way, the truth and the life.

Amen.

Father, in you I put my hope.
You sent Jesus, your Son,
to open for us a way of salvation
into the hope of eternal life.
Thank you.

Amen.

You have promised us
an inheritance as your children, Father God.
You accept us as your adopted children and heirs.
This is my hope.

Amen.

Thank you, Jesus,
that you are the foundation on which we can build.
Our hope is in you, our rock,
our fortress and our strength.

Amen.

Father God,
you have promised never to leave us or forsake us.
This gives us wonderful hope.
We know your Holy Spirit comforts and guides us.

Amen.

Lord God, you have overcome the world.
The victory is yours alone.
Our hope is steadfast and sure.

Amen.

To close

Leader The Lord himself goes before you, and will be with
you. Do not be afraid or discouraged.

(Deuteronomy 31:8)

Group *Our hope is in you, Lord.*

Worship songs

Faithful One
Brian Doerksen

Faithful One, so unchanging,
Ageless One, you're my rock of peace.
Lord of all, I depend on you,
I call out to you again and again,
I call out to you again and again.

You are my rock in times of trouble,
you lift me up when I fall down.
All through the storm your love is the anchor,
my hope is in you alone.

The Lord's my shepherd
from The Scottish Psalter

The Lord's my shepherd, I'll not want.
He makes me down to lie
in pastures green. He leadeth me
the quiet waters by.

My soul he doth restore again,
and me to walk doth make
within the paths of righteousness,
e'en for his own name's sake.

Yea' though I walk in death's dark vale,
yet will I fear none ill.
For thou art with me, and thy rod
and staff me comfort still.

My table thou hast furnishèd
in presence of my foes:
my head thou dost with oil anoint,
and my cup overflows.

Goodness and mercy all my life
shall surely follow me.
And in God's house for evermore
my dwelling-place shall be.

Further activity

Dictionary definition of HOPE:
'To cherish a desire for good, with the expectation of fulfilment' or 'Confident anticipation'.

Dictionary definition of DESPAIR:
'To be without hope.'

As believers, we say, 'Our hope is in the Lord'. That means we cherish a desire for good, with expectation of fulfilment and confident anticipation, in the Lord!

Without God there is no hope, only despair.

With the above definition in mind, continue with the activity.

Closing words

Hope is the anchor for the soul, firm and secure. Without hope, there is only despair. Jesus has gone before us – this is our hope. The Bible reassures us – this is our hope. God has given us this hope. May this seed send down deep roots which hold us firm in all our doubts, uncertainties, sorrows and disappointments. Let us cling to hope. Amen.

Salvation belongs to our God

Words and Music: Adrian Howard and Pat Turner

2. And we, the redeemed, shall be strong
   in purpose and unity,
   declaring aloud,
   praise and glory, wisdom and thanks,
   honour and power and strength.

Faithful One

Words and Music: Brian Doerksen

Faith - ful One, so un-chang - ing,

Age - less One, you're my rock of peace.

Lord of all, I de - pend on you,

I call out to you a-gain and a - gain,

I call out to you a-gain and a -

The Lord's my shepherd

Words: 'The Scottish Psalter'
Music: melody by Jessie Seymour Irvine

CRIMOND CM

2. My soul he doth restore again,
and me to walk doth make
within the paths of righteousness,
e'en for his own name's sake.

3. Yea, though I walk in death's dark vale,
yet will I fear none ill.
For thou art with me, and thy rod
and staff me comfort still.

4. My table thou hast furnishèd
in presence of my foes:
my head thou dost with oil anoint,
and my cup overflows.

5. Goodness and mercy all my life
shall surely follow me.
And in God's house for evermore
my dwelling-place shall be.

SESSION 9

Notes for Leader

Session 9: Family Worship (all-age)

THEME: FRIENDS

Introduction to theme

Abraham was a friend of God; Jesus says we can be his friends – what a privilege! How can we be friends with Jesus? What is a friend? This session, for people of all ages, uses the basic format for worship, but includes activities and creative ideas for younger members of the group, and responses which they can join in with.

It is suggested that, if children have friends in need of prayer, you ask before the meeting if they would agree to pray for their friends during the prayer time!

Resources required

You will need enough copies of the session for your group.

Worship songs:

These will be found on Album 2, tracks 13-16.

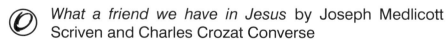 *What a friend we have in Jesus* by Joseph Medlicott Scriven and Charles Crozat Converse

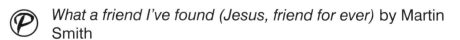 *What a friend I've found (Jesus, friend for ever)* by Martin Smith

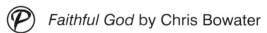 *Faithful God* by Chris Bowater

 Meditation track – *Dreamscape*

For activity 1:
- long piece of paper with clues to verse
- felt pen.

 For activity 2:
- large sheet of newsprint or wallpaper
- copies of the body parts on page 97 or life-size copies, depending on your activity
- glue
- large felt pen
- blindfold.

 Meditation and listening to God
- sheets of paper
- pens and pencils.

Preparation

 Reading from the Psalms

After reading Psalm 122 together, talk to the group about how the Psalm applies to us:

This Psalm tells us about going somewhere. We use our feet to go places, to be with our friends.

- How do we use feet? (Encourage the children to stamp their feet.)

The Psalm tells us about people coming together to praise the Lord. We use our voices to praise God. 'Hallelujah' is a good word to say.

- How do we use our voices? (Encourage the children to shout 'Hallelujah!')

The Psalm tells us to bless our friends with peace.

- Let's use our hands to show that we can be friends in peace. (Encourage everyone to shake hands with each other.)

 Further activities

Activity 1: deciphering a Bible verse

Ask two children or adults to hold up the verse clues (see page 96) on a long strip of paper so that it can be seen by the group. You will need a black felt pen to fill in the words.

Verse: Greater love has no one than this, that he lay down his life for his friends (John 15:13).

Activity 2: body parts

You will need the large sheet of paper, a felt pen, glue, and the body parts page 97 (life-size if you do option a, or copies of the page of drawings for option b, with a smaller drawing of a body shape).

a) Ask the smallest member of the group to lie down on a large piece of paper on the floor, and draw a rough body shape around them. Asking for volunteers, blindfold one, giving them a piece of the body (mouth, eyes, ears, etc.) to place on the body outline. As they attempt to do this, discuss with the group what friends can do with this part of the body – the mouth can talk, encourage, and thank; the ear can listen and so on. Once all the pieces have been placed on the body outline, (to some amusement, if the eye is on the knee and the foot on the tummy!) ask the children to glue them in the right places.

b) If space is limited or if a) is impractical, use a smaller outline and pin to an upright board or wall. The parts can still be positioned by blindfolded members of the group and then glued in position.

Activity 1: deciphering a Bible verse

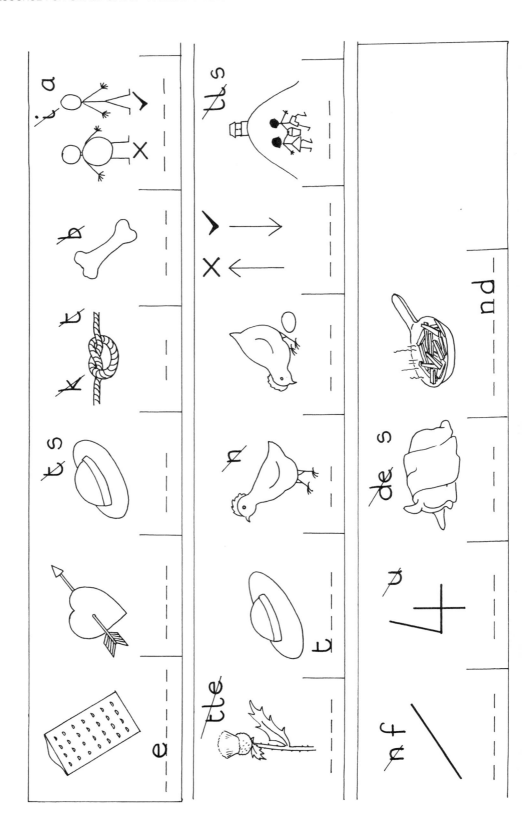

Activity 2: body parts

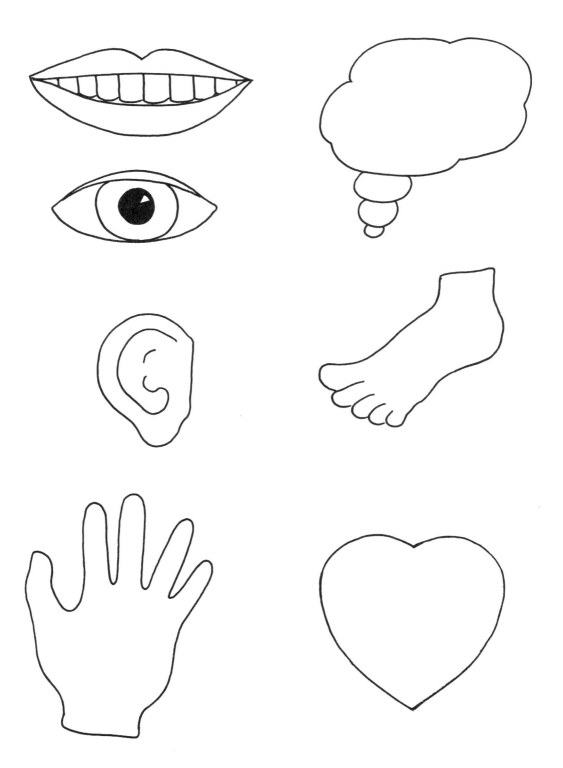

Meditation and listening to God

Use the poem *No Matter What* by Jane Amey. Suggested time for meditation: 1-2 minutes.

After the meditation time, give each person a piece of paper and a pen or pencil. The younger children can work with a family member or friend. Encourage them to write a letter to Jesus, imagining him as a penfriend or the friend with whom they share everything. If people would like to share their letters, give an opportunity for them to read aloud to the group.

Worship Session 9

THEME: FRIENDS

Opening words

Leader But now in Christ Jesus you who once were far away have been brought near through the blood of Christ.

Group *Because of Jesus, we can call God our friend.*

Worship song

What a friend we have in Jesus
Joseph Medlicott Scriven

What a friend we have in Jesus,
all our sins and griefs to bear!
What a privilege to carry
everything to him in prayer!
O what peace we often forfeit,
O what needless pain we bear,
all because we do not carry
everything to God in prayer!

Have we trials and temptations?
Is there trouble anywhere?
We should never be discouraged:
take it to the Lord in prayer!
Can we find a friend so faithful,
who will all our sorrows share?
Jesus knows our ev'ry weakness –
take it to the Lord in prayer!

Are we weak and heavy-laden,
cumbered with a load of care?
Jesus is our only refuge,
take it to the Lord in prayer!
Do thy friends despise, forsake thee?
Take it to the Lord in prayer!
In his arms he'll take and shield thee,
thou wilt find a solace there.

Reading from the Psalms

Leader I rejoiced with those who said to me,
'Let us go to the house of the Lord.'

Group *Let us go to the house of the Lord.*

Leader Our feet are standing in your gates, O Jerusalem.
Jerusalem is built like a city
that is like a close community,
where people come together to praise the Lord,
to praise the name of the Lord.

Group *Let us come together to praise the name of the Lord.*

Leader Pray for the peace of Jerusalem.
May those who love you be secure.
May there be peace within your walls
and security within your buildings!
For the sake of my brothers and friends,
I will say, 'Peace be within you.'

Group *Let us say to each other, 'Peace be within you.'*

Leader For the sake of the house of the Lord our God,
I will seek your prosperity.

Group *Let us ask God's blessing on our friends.*

(Based on Psalm 122)

Leader talks about the Psalm.

To close

Leader But now in Christ Jesus you who once were far away have been brought near through the blood of Christ.

Group *Because of Jesus, we can call God our friend.*

Activity 1: deciphering a Bible verse

Bible reading (Group member)

My command is this: Love each other as I have loved you. Greater love has no one than this, that he lay down his life for his friends. You are my friends if you do what I command. I no longer call you servants, because a servant does not know his master's business. Instead, I have called you friends, for everything that I learned from my Father; I have made known to you. You did not choose me, but I chose you and appointed you to go and bear fruit – fruit that will last. Then the Father will give you whatever you ask in my name. This is my command: Love each other.

(John 15:12 17)

Activity 2: body parts

Meditation and listening to God

Thought for meditation:

Leader (or member of group) reads the following poem:

Poem: *No matter what* by Jane Amey

No matter what,

no matter when,

I know he died for me,

that I could then be called God's friend:

he died to set me free.

In all the mess and muddle of

this stressful busy life,

when all around are wars and hurt

and tales of grief and strife,

I wonder whether hope lives on?

It's sometimes hard to grasp.

But every time I ask my Lord,

the answers come back fast.

No matter what, no matter when,

his life he gives to me.

For Jesus truly is my friend,

he wants to help me be.

Leader The Bible talks about Abraham being God's friend because he believed in God. Let's spend a few moments thinking about being a friend of God, or Jesus.

Prayer and praise

Leader Dear Lord Jesus,
thank you that you are the perfect friend.
Help me, Lord, to bless and not to curse;
my eyes to see a friend in need,
and my hands to help them in trouble.
Make my ears ready to listen,
my heart quick to love and care. Amen.

Worship songs

What a friend I've found
(Jesus, friend for ever)
Martin Smith

What a friend I've found,

closer than a brother.

I have felt your touch,

more intimate than lovers.

Jesus, Jesus,

Jesus, friend for ever.

What a hope I've found,

more faithful than a mother.

It would break my heart,

to ever lose each other.

© *1996 Curious? Music UK/Kingsway's Thankyou Music*

Faithful God
Chris Bowater

Faithful God, faithful God,

all-sufficient one, I worship you.

Shalom my peace,

my strong deliverer,

I lift you up,

faithful God.

Continue with prayers for friends of people in the group, encouraging young people to participate.

Closing words

Read the prayer from the Prayer and Praise section together.

What a friend we have in Jesus

Words: Joseph Medlicott Scriven
Music: Charles Crozat Converse

WHAT A FRIEND (CONVERSE) 87 87 D

1. What a friend we have in Je - sus,

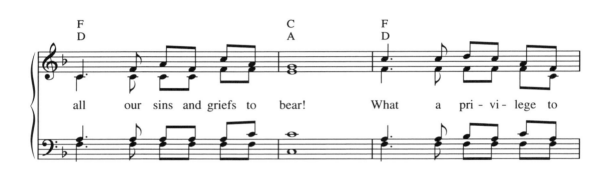

all our sins and griefs to bear! What a pri - vi - lege to

car - ry ev - 'ry - thing to him in prayer!

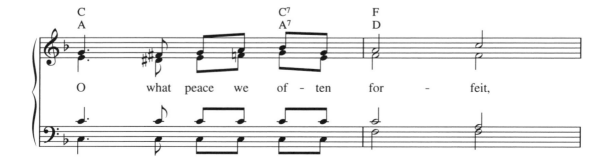

O what peace we of - ten for - feit,

O what need-less pain we bear, all be-cause we do not

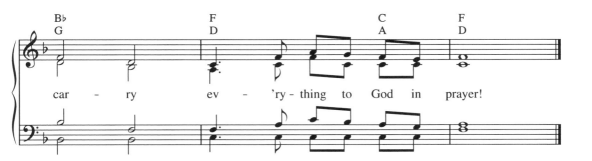

car - ry ev - 'ry-thing to God in prayer!

2. Have we trials and temptations?
   Is there trouble anywhere?
   We should never be discouraged:
   take it to the Lord in prayer!
   Can we find a friend so faithful,
   who will all our sorrows share?
   Jesus knows our ev'ry weakness –
   take it to the Lord in prayer!

3. Are we weak and heavy-laden,
   cumbered with a load of care?
   Jesus is our only refuge,
   take it to the Lord in prayer!
   Do thy friends despise, forsake thee?
   Take it to the Lord in prayer!
   In his arms he'll take and shield thee,
   thou wilt find a solace there.

What a friend I've found
Jesus, friend for ever

Words and Music: Martin Smith

1. What a friend I've found, clo-ser than a bro-ther.

I have felt your touch, more in-ti-mate than lo-vers.

Je - sus, Je - sus,

Je - sus, friend for e - ver.

2. What a hope I've found,
   more faithful than a mother.
   It would break my heart,
   to ever lose each other.

Faithful God

Words and Music: Chris Bowater

SESSION 10

Notes for Leader

Session 10: Social Awareness, Specific Issues

THEME: TIME AND TECHNOLOGY

Introduction to theme

Looking at our priorities for use of time and the concept that new technology will give us 'more time', the questions arise: 'for what?' and 'does it?' It is amazing how many Christians are more knowledgeable about TV serials and presenters, film stars, pop singers and computers, than about the Bible and the 'Law of the Lord', or the Gospel truths. The new technology and the media affect us all. This session gives the group a chance to look at their time, their lifestyle and priorities, and is intended to lead into discussion and positive action that will affect the needs in the community.

Resources required

You will need enough copies of the session for your group.

Worship songs:

These will be found on Album 2, tracks 17-20.

 Lord, I lift your name on high (You came from heaven to earth) by Rick Founds

 Lord, we long for you (Heal our nation) by Trish Morgan, Ray Goudie, Ian Townend, Dave Bankhead

 Make me a channel of your peace by Sebastian Temple

 Meditation track – *Ambience*

Extracts from *Breaking the Rules* by Eddie Askew.

  Paper and pens/pencils.

 Copies of situations for discussion.

 3 copies of the sketch, *Moving In* by Pat Turner.

Preparation

 Start the session by reading this quote from *Breaking the Rules* by Eddie Askew:

We can see the face of Jupiter, but does it help us to see more clearly the face of our neighbour, or his need? While we reach into space, people stay hungry, homeless and sick. Sometimes, for all the notice we take of them, they might live on a different planet. But they are here with us now. How much technology do we need to reach out and touch them?

 Meditation and listening to God

Thought for meditation: Repeat the passage above from *Breaking the Rules* by Eddie Askew, then continue with his poem:

Lord,
help me see
that if technology can't cope
with your demands
for justice, mercy –
I won't mention love,
that's just too much to ask –
then something's wrong.
The need is here.

And reaching out beyond our world
won't help.
You ask me
not to reach for the stars
but just to walk
the harder journey
to my neighbour
down the road.

During our time of meditation let's consider the time we spend with 'new technology' – television, videos, computer, the internet – compared to the time we spend with those in need of our care and friendship – even time given to the Lord. How has it affected our lifestyle?

Suggested time for meditation: 3-5 minutes.

After the time of meditation, spend a short time discussing the value of new technology, asking the group for positive and negative feelings, thinking of the concerns voiced by Eddie Askew in the paragraph quoted.

 Prayer and praise

Encourage each member of the group to write a personal prayer using pens and paper provided, making a commitment of time to be spent with God and in care and service within the community. These prayers need not be shared in the group, but it is encouraging if individuals report back in subsequent weeks on what they have been able to do, however insignificant they may consider it. The group might be able to help with ideas if some members want to help but are not sure how to make contacts.

Further activities

Activity 1

Divide the group into threes or fours, with access to paper and pens/pencils. Give each group the list of suggested discussion topics, (see over).

Your group may be very diverse in their use of 'new technology' so the topic could include all aspects of the media – magazines, newspapers, radio as well as TV, videos, computers, etc. Give time for each group to share some of the thoughts they have written down at the end of the period.

This is not meant to be a session to make the group feel guilty, but to make each person aware of aspects of lifestyle, where encroaching technology or media may affect relationships, communication, caring and worship. People may want to experiment with a week of no TV, videos, computers, radios, to see what happens to their time!

Activity 2

Use the sketch *Moving In* by Pat Turner. Even within the church we can become 'too busy' to care for people, or spend time with Jesus. Time and priorities are big issues. This sketch could be performed with practice, or read by members of the group. The issues raised can then be discussed in the group session.

Activity 1

Situations for discussion

1 Read Acts 8:26-31

Imagine you are Philip, and you realise that this is an encounter which may take a long time. In this day and age, our big complaint is, 'I haven't got time', or 'I don't know where the time goes', or 'If only I had the time'. Has time-saving technology been any help?

Discuss the reality of the following alternatives:

- Philip could suggest that they make an appointment for another day when it was more convenient, i.e. in a comfortable office or over a meal. Would this be a good idea?

- Philip remembers that the big football game is starting on TV and unless he gets home soon, he will miss it – he has to make a decision. What are the options?

- Philip suggests that the eunuch e-mail any questions he has about the passages to him, after he gets home. This will save them both time. Philip will respond by e-mail. Would this affect the result of their meeting?

2 Read Mark 6:32-36

Instead of the crowd running around the lake to meet Jesus, they know it will be on the local TV news during the evening, or they can watch a video of his previous gatherings. They stay home. Discuss:

a) How this would affect the disciples?

b) How this would affect the crowd?

c) How this would affect Jesus' ministry?

3 Read Matthew 7:13-14

Discuss 'narrow' and 'wide' roads as lifestyles. Why would Jesus warn us to beware of the 'broad road'? Consider this in the light of TV programmes; list which ones you think Jesus might enjoy and which he might think questionable. Would you feel comfortable watching TV shows and videos with Jesus staying at your house? Discuss your views!

4 Read Ecclesiastes 3:9-14

'A time for everything.' Discuss how things have changed in your lifetime and why. Consider how you spend your time and what your priorities are. With labour-saving devices, faster transport, etc. there is now more time for visiting the sick and elderly, caring for the lonely and sad, welcoming the stranger, sharing the Gospel — is this your experience?

5 Read 2 John, verse 12

We have telephones, fax machines, e-mail and letters. How do we use these to keep in touch? Do we like them as an alternative to visiting and are they good alternatives? Discuss from your own experiences.

Activity 2

MOVING IN
Pat Turner

The cast

J   the stranger

John

Brian   enthusiastic, active, smiling Christian

Props

A Bible

A large diary

J Hi John!

John Oh, I see you've moved in.

J Yes. Came as soon as you called.

John I called?

J Got the word yesterday so I came round and - well - the door was open, so here I am!

John Oh. Right. I'd better show you around.

J It's OK, I know everything. Anyway, I've brought you something - a little moving-in present, you might say.

*(He presents **John** with a Bible)*

John A book?

J Just one I wrote earlier.

*(**John** is puzzled. He looks at the book and looks at the person but can't work it out)*

John You know, I'm glad you came actually. I feel I can trust you somehow and . . . Can I tell you something?

J You want to talk; I want to listen.

John It's a bit embarrassing really. I've got this problem at work. The boss is . . .

Both giving me/you a hard time . . .

John and he's . . .

J deliberately . . .

John giving me all the rotten jobs just out of –

J jealousy.

John spite.

J jealousy.

John No, you don't understand the situation.

J Let's just say I see it differently.

John You know him?

J Very well.

John He didn't mention you.

J He hasn't met me.

(**John** is confused)

J Anyway, it's as good as sorted, so don't worry about it. Worrying doesn't improve anything.

John Yeah. You're right . . . Oh, look here, I'm taking all your time. You must have things to do. I talk too much.

J I like to talk.

(Pause)

John I'm really glad you've moved in. I think we'll get on well. Don't you want to unpack?

J Later perhaps. I'd rather keep talking. Tell me about yourself.

John There is one thing I'd like to ask you about . . .

J Fire away.

John I had a bit of an odd day yesterday. I had the strangest urge to go to church and . . . to cut a long story short . . .

J You wanted to be a Christian.

John *(Surprised)* Yes! I did . . . but I don't think I understood it all.

J No?

John I always thought God was up there somewhere watching – all seeing, all knowing . . . *(Looks at him, confused)* . . . but they were talking about some sort of relationship – like you could just talk to him – well, like I'm talking to you now.

J It's all in the book. Everything you need to know.

*(**Brian** enters enthusiastically)*

Brian John!

John Oh, it's my mate from church.

Brian Hi John! Doing alright? *(Doesn't really want an answer so doesn't bother listening)*

John Actually no . . .

Brian Good. Now, I've brought something for you . . . *(Sees the stranger)*

John Let me introduce you to – er . . .

Brian Hi! *(Promptly ignores him)*

J Hi Brian!

Brian Now John – the question is, what book does every Christian need?

J The Bible.

Brian *(Hasn't heard)* The Diary! *(He gives **John** a substantial diary. **John** has to put the Bible down in order to take it)* Service for the Lord now, mate.

John Of course . . . Anything for the . . . Lord

Brian Now, as a newcomer we recommend that you get stuck in – feel useful – feel part of the team. Be a 'doer', not just a hearer, John. You'll really find true happiness when you're doing, doing, doing.

John Doing, doing, doing. Right!

Brian So here we go. Monday, children's work; Tuesday, choir practice; Wednesday is work-on-the-building night; Thursday is the Entertainments Committee – nothing like a fun night out for making new friends, eh John?

John That only leaves me with Friday!

Brian Oh yes, Friday . . . the youth work, of course! Hope you can drive – we need people for transport.

J You've forgotten something.

Brian Have I? *(Puzzled)* Oh yes! Coffee rota! . . . See you later, John, and don't forget . . .
*(**Brian** and **John** point to each other)*

Both Doing, doing, doing!

*(**Brian** leaves. **John** is pleased with his diary)*

John Smart diary, eh?

J Yeah.

John Best fill in the dates then.

J Yeah.

John Got a pen I can borrow?

J No actually.

John Oh. I'll look in my room then – bound to be one somewhere.

J Can't it wait?

John Not after that list! Need to get it all down while I remember . . . I'm gonna really work at this, you know. I'm gonna do it right – be committed – get stuck in.

*(He is about to go to his room. **J** picks up the Bible)*

J You forgot this. *(Holds it out to him)*

John *(Looks)* I'll pick it up later – bit tied up now. *(He reads his diary as he leaves, then stops in his tracks)* Oh – I'll be out tomorrow night . . .

Both Doing, doing, doing.

John Yes . . . Don't expect we'll see much of each other now – commitments and all. Still – make yourself at home. *(**John** leaves)*

J *(Looks at the Bible in his hands, looks around the room, looks to the place where **John** left. Quietly . . .)* Actually, John, I'm thinking of moving out.

Worship Session 10

THEME: TIME AND TECHNOLOGY

Opening words

Leader Test me, O Lord, and try me,
examine my heart and my mind,
for your love is ever before me
and I walk continually in your truth.
(Psalm 26:2-3)

Group *Blessed are all who fear the Lord,*
who walk in his ways.

Leader Jesus said, 'I was hungry and you gave me
nothing to eat,
I was thirsty and you gave me nothing to drink,
I was a stranger and you did not invite me in,
I needed clothes and you did not clothe me,
I was sick and in prison and you did not look after me.'

Group *Lord, when did we see you hungry or thirsty,*
or a stranger or needing clothes,
or sick or in prison and did not help you?

Leader 'I tell you the truth,
whatever you did not do for one of the least
of these people,
you did not do for me.'
(Matthew 25:42-45)

Group *Test me, O Lord, and try me,*
examine my heart and my mind.

Worship song

**Lord, I lift your name on high
(You came from heaven to earth)**
Rick Founds

Lord, I lift your name on high;

Lord, I love to sing your praises.

I'm so glad you're in my life;

I'm so glad you came to save us.

Lord, I lift your name on high;

Lord, I love to sing your praises.

I'm so glad you're in my life;

I'm so glad you came to save us.

You came from heaven to earth

to show the way,

from the earth to the cross,

my debt to pay,

from the cross to the grave,

from the grave to the sky,

Lord, I lift your name on high.

© 1989 Maranatha! Music/CopyCare

Reading from the Psalms

Leader Blessed is the man
who does not walk in the counsel of the wicked
or stand in the way of sinners,
or sit in the seat of mockers.

Group *His delight is in the law of the Lord*
and on his law he meditates day and night.

Leader He is like a tree planted by steams of water
which yields its fruit in season,
and whose leaf does not wither.
Whatever he does prospers.

Group *The Lord watches over the way of the righteous.*

(From Psalm 1)

Leader Lord, who may dwell in your sanctuary?
Who may live on your holy hill?

Group *He whose walk is blameless*
and who does what is righteous,
who speaks the truth from his heart.

Leader The one with no slander on his tongue,
who does his neighbour no wrong
and casts no slur on his fellow man.

Group *Those who honour the people who fear the Lord,*
who keep his law even when it hurts.

Leader The man who lends his money without
expecting interest
and does not accept a bribe against the innocent.

Group *He who does these things will never be shaken.*

(Adapted from Psalm 15)

Leader How can one keep one's ways pure?
By living according to your word, O Lord.

Group *I have hidden your word in my heart
that I might not sin against you.*

Leader Direct me in the path of your commands,
for there I find delight.

Group *Turn my eyes away from worthless things;
renew my life according to your word.*

(Adapted from Psalm 119)

Meditation and prayer

The thought for meditation is taken from *Breaking the Rules* by Eddie Askew.

During our time of meditation let's consider the time we spend with 'new technology' – television, videos, computer, the internet – compared to the time we spend with those in need of our care and friendship – even time given to the Lord. How has it affected our lifestyle?

Prayer and praise

Worship songs

Heal our nation
(Lord, we long for you)
Trish Morgan, Ray Goudie, Ian Townend and Dave Bankhead

Lord, we long for you to
move in power.
There's a hunger deep
within our hearts
to see healing in our nation.
Send your Spirit to revive us.

Heal our nation!
Heal our nation!
Heal our nation!
Pour out your Spirit on this land!

Lord, we hear your Spirit
coming closer,
a mighty wave to break
upon our land,
bringing justice and forgiveness.
God, we cry to you, 'Revive us!'

© *1986 Kingsway's Thankyou Music*

Make me a channel of your peace
Sebastian Temple

Make me a channel of your peace.
Where there is hatred,
let me bring your love.
Where there is injury, your pardon, Lord,
and where there's doubt,
true faith in you.

O Master, grant that I may never seek
so much to be consoled as to console,
to be understood as to understand,
to be loved, as to love with all my soul.

Make me a channel of your peace.
Where there's despair in life,
let me bring hope.
Where there is darkness, only light,
and where there's sadness, ever joy.

Make me a channel of your peace.
It is in pardoning that we are pardoned,
in giving of ourselves that we receive,
and in dying that we're born to eternal life.

Further activity

There is a list of discussion starters and a sketch, *Moving In*, by Pat Turner.

This is not meant to be a session to make anyone feel guilty, but to make each person aware of aspects of lifestyle, where encroaching technology or media may affect relationships, communication, caring and worship.

People may want to experiment with a week of no TV, videos, computers, radios, to see what happens to their time!

Closing words

Leader Lord, accept our prayers of commitment
as a genuine expression of our desire to care.
We want to see the people in our community through your eyes, to see the needs that you see.
Whatever we do, Lord,
we want to do it as if we were doing it for you.
Lord, we pray that we use our time wisely;
our energy and ability in the right channels.
Above all, we want to serve you and worship you.
In Jesus' name.

Amen.

Lord, I lift your name on high
You came from heaven to earth

Words and Music: Rick Founds

Lord, I lift your name on high;

Lord, I love to sing your prai - ses.

I'm so glad you're in my life;

I'm so glad you came to save us.

You came from hea - ven to earth to show the way,

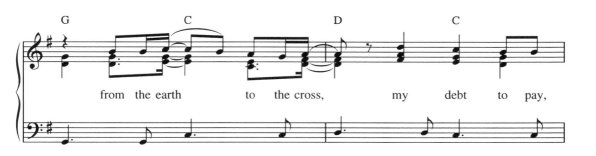

from the earth to the cross, my debt to pay,

from the cross to the grave, from the grave to the sky,

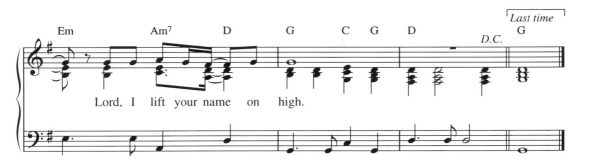

Lord, I lift your name on high.

Lord, we long for you
Heal our nation

Words and Music: Trish Morgan, Ray Goudie,
Ian Townend and Dave Bankhead

2. Lord, we hear your Spirit coming closer,
   a mighty wave to break upon our land,
   bringing justice and forgiveness.
   God, we cry to you, 'Revive us!'

Make me a channel of your peace

Words and Music: Sebastian Temple, based on the Prayer of St. Francis

much to be con - soled as to con - sole, to be
un - der - stood, as to un - der - stand, to be
loved, as to love with all my soul.

2. Make me a channel of your peace.
   Where there's despair in life, let me bring hope.
   Where there is darkness, only light,
   and where there's sadness, ever joy.

3. Make me a channel of your peace.
   It is in pardoning that we are pardoned,
   in giving of ourselves that we receive,
   and in dying that we're born to eternal life.

Acknowledgements

The publishers wish to express their gratitude to the following for permission to include copyright material in this book:

Mr Ronnie Barclay for the extracts from his father's book *The Plain Man looks at the Beatitudes*, published by Collins Fantasia Books.

CopyCare, P.O. Box 77, Hailsham, East Sussex BN27 3EF (HYPERLINK mail to: music@copycare.com) for the songs *As we are gathered* © 1979 Word's Spirit of Praise Music; *Jesus is King* © 1982 Word's Spirit of Praise Music; *Peace like a river* © 1989 Ampelos Music; *Faithful One* © 1989 Mercy/Vineyard Publishing and *Lord, I lift your name on high* © 1989 Maranatha! Music.

Curtis Brown Group Ltd, Haymarket House, 28/29 Haymarket, London SW1Y 4SP for the extract from *God is for real, man* by Carl Burke, published by Collins Fontana.

Hodder and Stoughton Ltd, 338 Euston Road, London NW1 3BH for the extracts from The New International Version of the Bible, © 1973, 1978, 1984 International Bible Society. All rights reserved. (NIV is a registered trademark of International Bible Society. UK trademark number 1448790)

Kingsway's Thankyou Music, P.O. Box 75, Eastbourne, East Sussex BN23 6NW, UK for the songs *Jesus, what a beautiful name* © 1995 Tanya Riches/Hillsong Music Australia; *Our confidence is in the Lord* © 1989 Kingway's Thankyou Music; *What a friend I've found* © 1996 Curious? Music UK (World-wide, excl. USA) and *Lord, we long for you* © 1986 Kingsway's Thankyou Music.

The Leprosy Mission International, 80 Windmill Road, Brentford, Middlesex TW8 0QH for the extracts from *Breaking the Rules* and *No Strange Land*, both by Eddie Askew.

Make Way Music, P.O. Box 263, Croydon, CR9 5AP, UK for the song *Peace to you* © 1988 Make Way Music. International copyright secured. All rights reserved.

OCP Publications, 5536 NE Hassalo, Portland, Oregon 97213, USA for the song *Make me a channel of your peace* © 1967. All rights reserved. Used by permission.

Sovereign Lifestyle Music Ltd, P.O. Box 356, Leighton Buzzard, Beds. LU7 8WP, UK for the song *Faithful God* © 1990.

Sovereign Music UK, P.O. Box 356, Leighton Buzzard, Beds. LU7 8WP, UK for the song *Salvation belongs to our God* © 1985 Restoration Music Ltd.

Every effort has been made to trace the owners of copyright material and we hope that no copyright has been infringed. Pardon is sought and apology made if the contrary be the case, and a correction will be made in any reprint of this book.